25↑

July 26, 1964

To Helen and Hugh, dear friends to me always, and who initiated me to the joys of a ketch, and the charms and mystery of the Isles.

Affectionately,

Louise

CLIPPER SHIP

AMERICA'S FAMOUS AND FAST-SAILING QUEENS OF THE SEA

Copy of a clipper-ship sailing card

E. TRAIN & CO.

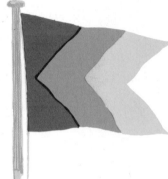

GRINNEL MINTURN & CO.

GLIDDEN & WILLIAMS LINE

WELLS & EMANUEL

CROCKER & STURGIS

CLIPPER SHIP

AMERICA'S FAMOUS AND FAST-SAILING QUEENS OF THE SEA

Written and Illustrated by

John O'Hara Cosgrave II

The Macmillan Company, New York
Collier-Macmillan Ltd., London
1963

The *Frontier West Books* have been prepared under the general editorship of Glen Dines

Clipper ship sailing to windward

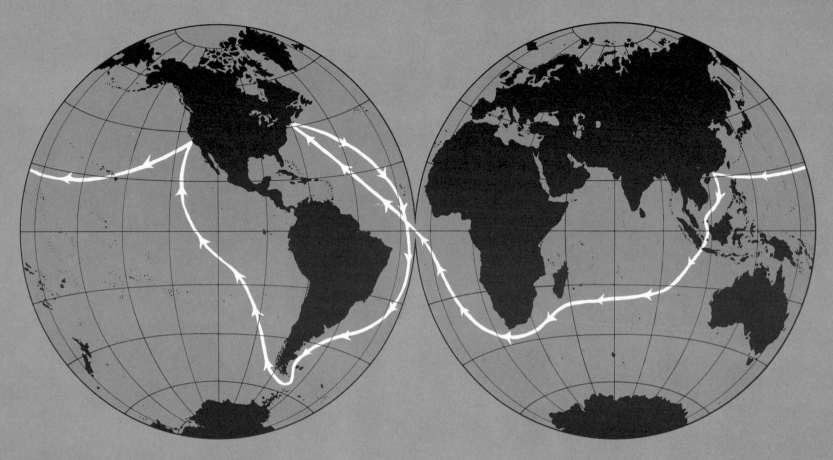

Many of the clipper ships sailed around the world on each passage. They would leave New York loaded with passengers and equipment, discharge them at San Francisco, then sail in ballast to China, there load up with tea, proceed around the Cape of Good Hope, and cross the Atlantic to return to New York.

South Street, New York, 1851

HE clipper ship was an American invention, born of the necessity for speed. This most beautiful of all sailing ships evolved between 1845 and 1850, and had its great days of fast passages and record runs from 1848 to 1860.

The clipper, built mainly for speed, had a long, narrow hull and a set of tall masts that could carry enormous clouds of canvas. Under ideal conditions, a fast clipper could make 18 knots (equal to 20¾ land miles per hour), a respectable speed for a ship even today. A few exceptional passages down the East Coast, around the southern tip of South America, and on up to San Francisco took less than a hundred days, with an average speed of 6¼ knots.

From 1840 to 1850, before the prime of American clipper ships, the small China-tea clippers flourished. On these the designers and crews "learned the ropes."

When gold was discovered in California, thousands of people were in a hurry to get to the mines. They had to carry tools and food with them. Crossing the continent in a covered wagon was slow and hazardous, and space for equipment was limited.

Some took a steamer from New York to the Isthmus of Panama, crossed the disease-infested jungle on foot or by donkey, then boarded another steamer to San Francisco. Little food or equipment could be taken along on this route, so the clippers took the lead in the gold-rush traffic, and their owners prospered. The average price for a passage from New York to San Francisco on one of the faster clippers was $1000, and some of the ships could carry a hundred passengers or more. Sometimes the entire cost of building a ship was paid off by her first voyage.

Clipper ship under construction

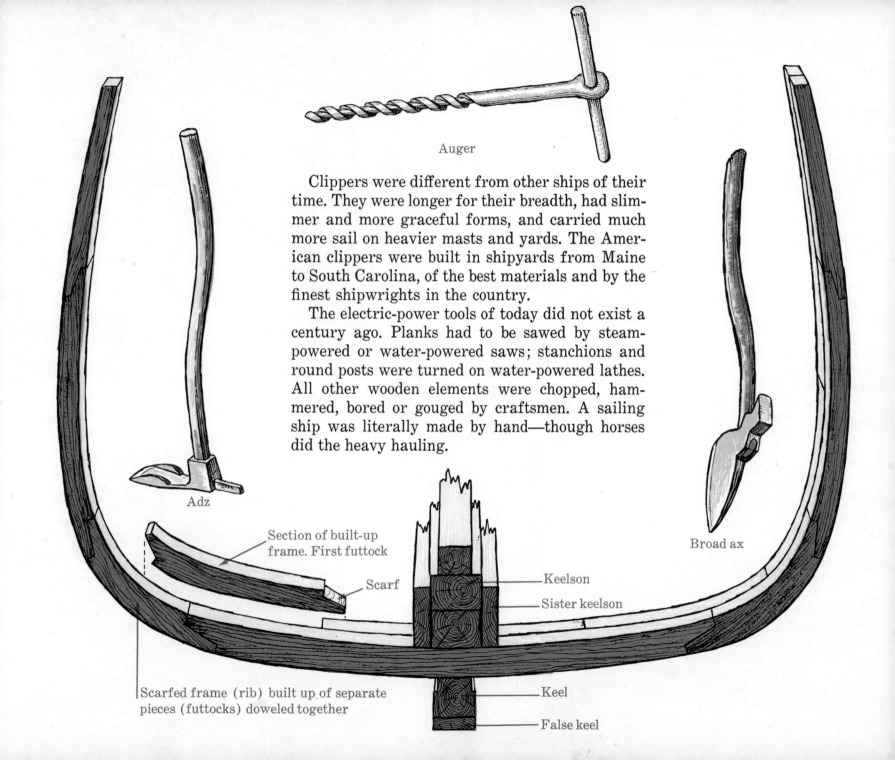

Auger

Clippers were different from other ships of their time. They were longer for their breadth, had slimmer and more graceful forms, and carried much more sail on heavier masts and yards. The American clippers were built in shipyards from Maine to South Carolina, of the best materials and by the finest shipwrights in the country.

The electric-power tools of today did not exist a century ago. Planks had to be sawed by steam-powered or water-powered saws; stanchions and round posts were turned on water-powered lathes. All other wooden elements were chopped, hammered, bored or gouged by craftsmen. A sailing ship was literally made by hand—though horses did the heavy hauling.

Adz

Broad ax

Section of built-up frame. First futtock

Scarf

Keelson

Sister keelson

Scarfed frame (rib) built up of separate pieces (futtocks) doweled together

Keel

False keel

The best way to show what a ship's lines look like is to make a lift half-model, then "take off" or "lay down" the lines. In the clipper-ship era, this was the method used by most ship designers. First, dowels were run through a stack of lifts, or layers of soft wood (1). This block was carved into the shape of half the vessel's hull (2); usually, the scale was 1/3 of an inch on the model to 1 foot on the actual ship.

The waterline (the level water reaches on the hull) depends on how much weight the ship is carrying. To draw sample waterlines, the designer pulled out dowels D and D' (1), separated the lifts (3) and traced their outlines on paper. On plans at right, waterlines are marked A, B and C.

To show the ship's sections, the model was doweled together again, measured off at regular intervals, then sawed into cross sections (4 and 5). The outlines of sections 1, 2, 3, etc., then were traced for the section plans. To save space and drawing time, naval architects show half the bow section and half the stern section, as on the opposite page. They also draw only one side of the hull's length, since port is exactly the reverse of starboard; here, both sides are drawn to give a complete view of waterlines.

To show the buttock lines, the model was reassembled, marked off at regular intervals, then sawed in lines parallel to its axis (6 and 7). When traced off, these are sections such as X, Y, and Z.

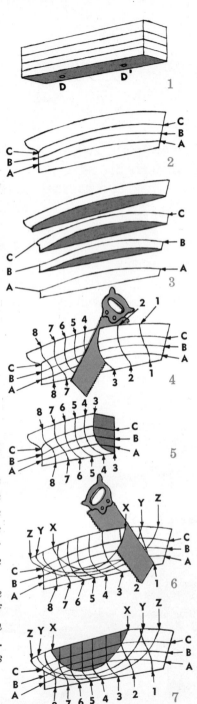

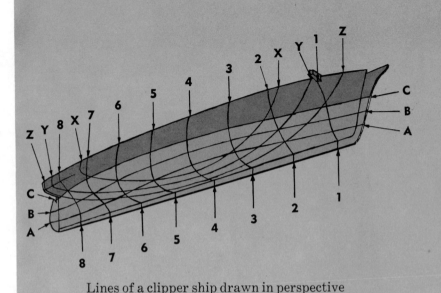

Lines of a clipper ship drawn in perspective

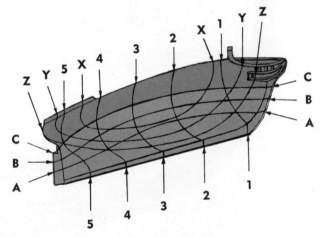

Lines of a full-bodied merchant ship drawn in perspective

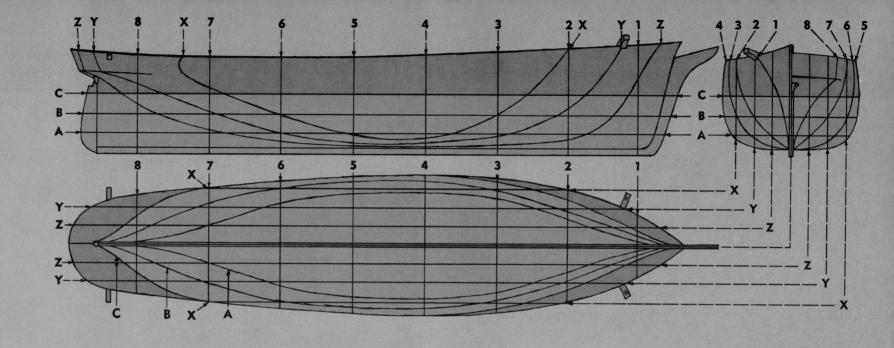

Lines of a clipper ship and a
full-bodied merchant ship

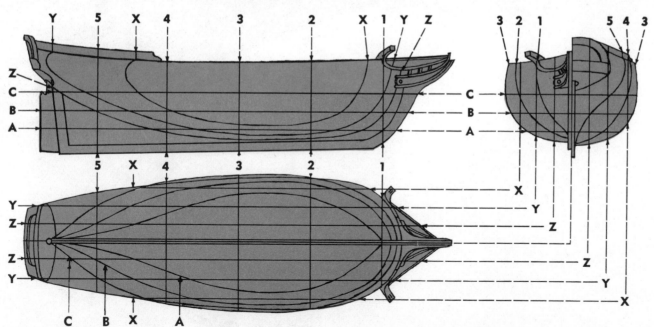

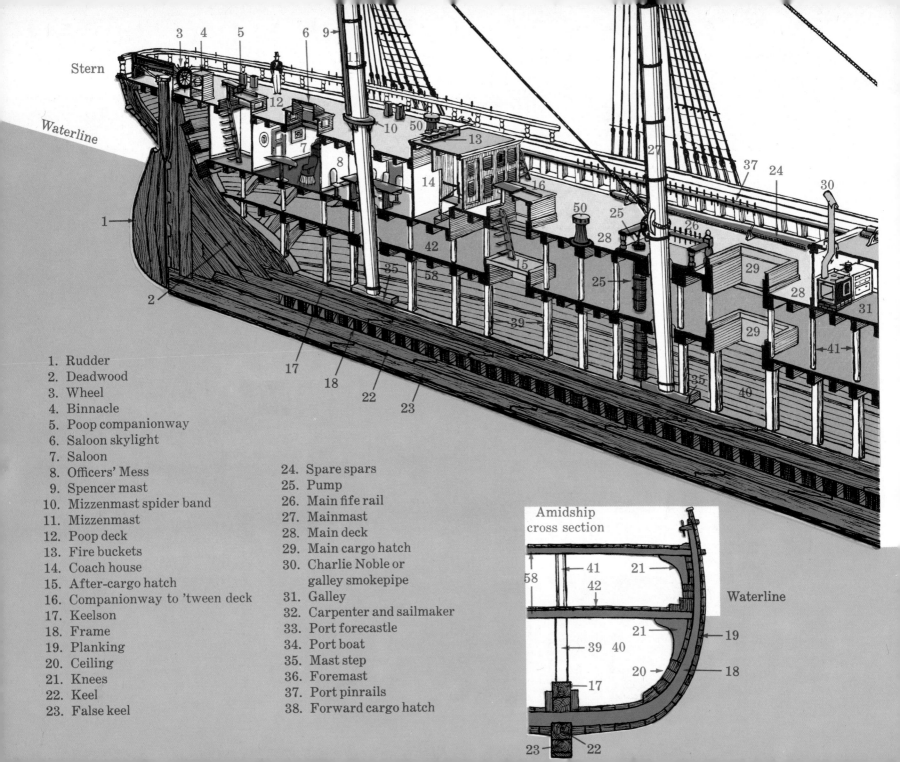

Stern

Waterline

1. Rudder
2. Deadwood
3. Wheel
4. Binnacle
5. Poop companionway
6. Saloon skylight
7. Saloon
8. Officers' Mess
9. Spencer mast
10. Mizzenmast spider band
11. Mizzenmast
12. Poop deck
13. Fire buckets
14. Coach house
15. After-cargo hatch
16. Companionway to 'tween deck
17. Keelson
18. Frame
19. Planking
20. Ceiling
21. Knees
22. Keel
23. False keel

24. Spare spars
25. Pump
26. Main fife rail
27. Mainmast
28. Main deck
29. Main cargo hatch
30. Charlie Noble or
    galley smokepipe
31. Galley
32. Carpenter and sailmaker
33. Port forecastle
34. Port boat
35. Mast step
36. Foremast
37. Port pinrails
38. Forward cargo hatch

Amidship
cross section

Waterline

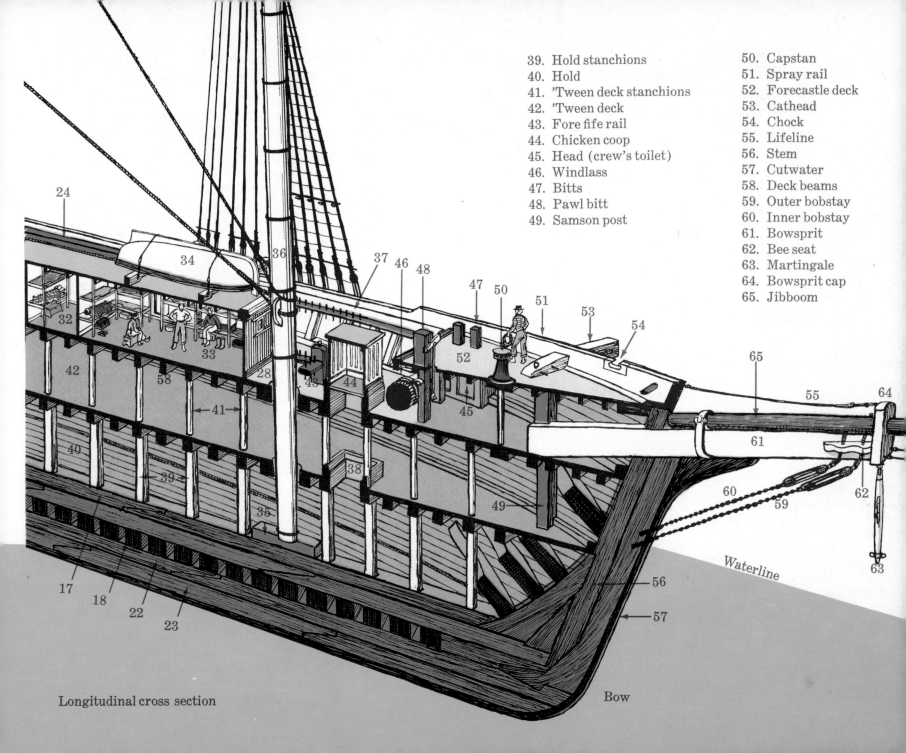

39. Hold stanchions
40. Hold
41. 'Tween deck stanchions
42. 'Tween deck
43. Fore fife rail
44. Chicken coop
45. Head (crew's toilet)
46. Windlass
47. Bitts
48. Pawl bitt
49. Samson post

50. Capstan
51. Spray rail
52. Forecastle deck
53. Cathead
54. Chock
55. Lifeline
56. Stem
57. Cutwater
58. Deck beams
59. Outer bobstay
60. Inner bobstay
61. Bowsprit
62. Bee seat
63. Martingale
64. Bowsprit cap
65. Jibboom

Longitudinal cross section

Bow

Waterline

When it came to building a clipper, the lines traced from the lift half-model were enlarged to full size on the floor of the mould loft. From these ship-sized plans, a mould (or pattern) of thin wood was cut for each rib, or frame. At the shipyard, the moulds were traced on the pieces of wood to be used for construction, which were then chopped or sawed into finished shape.

Shipyards were located on bays or rivers with water deep enough to float the vessel when it was finished. The clipper was built outdoors on slanting ways, stern to the water.

Only the best quality materials were used by the shipbuilders, mechanics, riggers and sailmakers because the whole fabric of a clipper would be subjected to extraordinary stress and strain. The keel, knees, and frames were built of oak; the planks, ceiling, and decks were of yellow pine, fastened with treenails (pronounced *trunnels*), which are hardwood dowels whose ends were split and wedged to make them hold better. Fancy decorative trim was of teak or mahogany. The masts and spars were made of pine, and on the largest vessels the lower masts were built-up—that is, they were constructed of many long pieces carefully fitted together and tightly bound with iron hoops.

The standing rigging (the shrouds, backstays, stays, and so on) was of hemp, which stretched readily and needed constant setting up, or tightening. Running rigging, braces, sheets, and some of the halliards were of Manila rope, a strong line even though made of hemp. The sails were cotton canvas, varying from the light cotton duck of the skysails to the stiff, boardlike storm staysails.

Bird's-eye view of a clipper ship

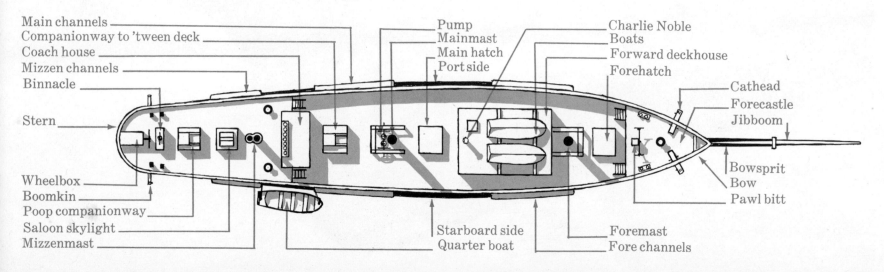

Main channels
Companionway to 'tween deck
Coach house
Mizzen channels
Binnacle

Stern

Wheelbox
Boomkin
Poop companionway
Saloon skylight
Mizzenmast

Pump
Mainmast
Main hatch
Port side

Starboard side
Quarter boat

Charlie Noble
Boats
Forward deckhouse
Forehatch

Cathead
Forecastle
Jibboom

Bowsprit
Bow
Pawl bitt

Foremast
Fore channels

Figurehead and bow of a clipper ship

Thin overlapping sheets of copper, tacked to the bottom of the ship, protected the hull from marine borers—such as worms and teredos—and kept grass, barnacles, and seaweed from adhering. Parasites like these would increase water friction, slowing up the ship.

When the hull and decks were completed, and the lower masts and bowsprit were stepped and stayed, the foreman gave the order for the ship to be slipped down the ways. Ship launchings in those days were not the gala occasions that they are today. When the ship started to move, the foreman would simply pour a bottle of rum on her deck and shout her name.

After the launching, the ship was towed to the rigger's dock, where the upper masts and their stays, the yards, jibboom and all rigging were added. At the same time, cabin and deck fittings were installed. All that remained was to ship a crew and bend the sails.

(Opposite page)—Forward section of ship on launching ways

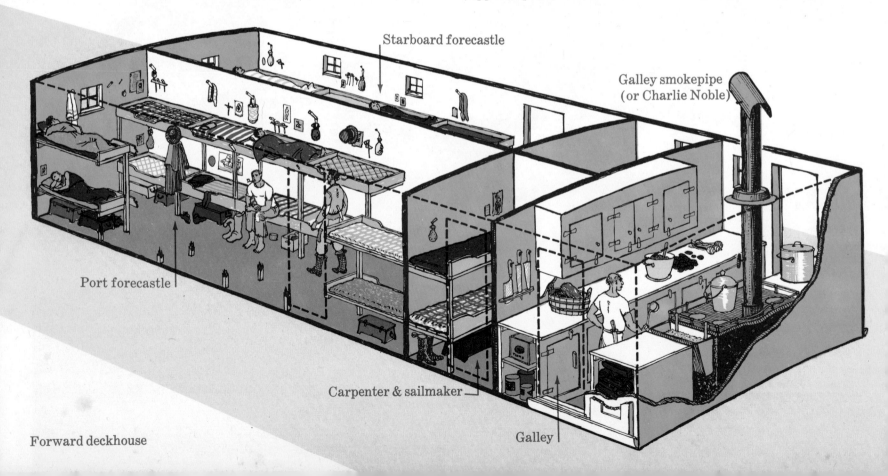

Starboard forecastle

Galley smokepipe
(or Charlie Noble)

Port forecastle

Carpenter & sailmaker

Galley

Forward deckhouse

The most exciting day aboard a ship was sailing day. With all cargo stowed and the hatches battened down (sealed and covered with canvas), supplies in the lazaret, the officers aboard in their shore-going clothes, the crew helped aboard after a brief spree on land, and the passengers shouting last farewells, the clipper was off to California and the gold fields! A fussy, puffing paddle-wheel tug pulled the ship out into the harbor. There, if the wind was favorable, sail was set and the ship came to life. There were creaks and groans as the yards moved on the masts, chirps and squeaks from the blocks as the water's roll shifted the lines in them. There was a deep hum like that of a vast aeolian harp: the wind in the rigging, every line and stay with its own sound, according to its length and tension. As the vessel pitched, the reef points slapped against the sails with little flapping sounds. The crew sang a chantey (pronounced *shanty*) as they heaved on sheets and halliards. It was a lucky ship that had a good chanteyman aboard, for the rhythm helped all hands to pull together and that lightened the load.

The odor of Stockholm tar (it smells like Noxzema) came from the rigging, and there was a delicate reek from the galley stove, which was burning off the coat of paint put on while the ship was tied up. In corners on deck and under the forecastle head, the sharp, unpleasant odor of bilge was lurking. The smell of bilge could be like stale water, spoiled sugar, rotten wood, mildew, and decay.

Throughout the vessel, the atmosphere would be tense as the crew sized up the mates and the mates made silent choices for their watches. The captain, standing at the break of the poop, might give the men a brief talk, saying mainly that he expected all hands to do their duty. And then the first mate would choose the first man for the port watch, the second mate would choose the next for his starboard watch, and so on, until the last man was assigned to a watch.

By this time the clipper was through the channel; the pilot climbed down the Jacob's ladder to a bobbing rowboat that would take him back to the pilot schooner. Now the ship was at sea, and the captain was the master of all hands.

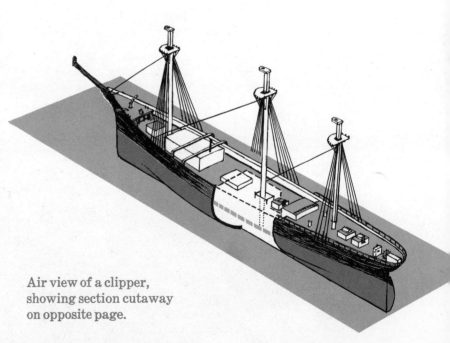

Air view of a clipper,
showing section cutaway
on opposite page.

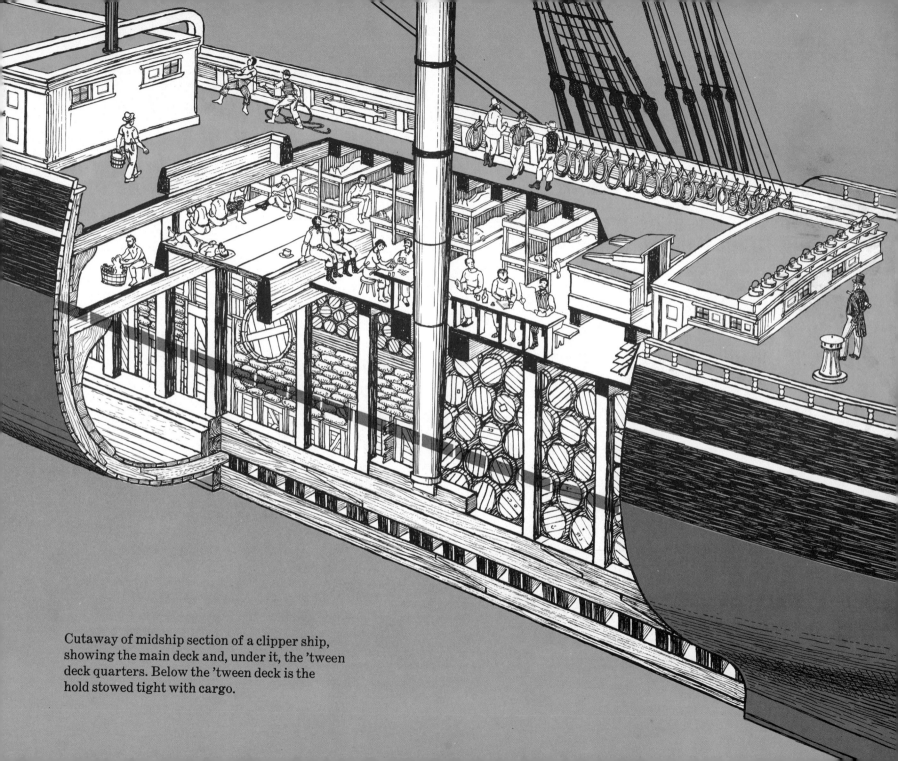

Cutaway of midship section of a clipper ship,
showing the main deck and, under it, the 'tween
deck quarters. Below the 'tween deck is the
hold stowed tight with cargo.

Chronometer

12
1
2
3
4
5
6

⟶○ A gale of wind
⟶○ Fresh breeze
⟶○ Moderate breeze
⟶○ Light breeze
⟶☼ Light variable airs
○ Calm
⟶⟶○ Fresh breeze with squalls

130° West of Greenwich

⟶☼ Part of day with fresh breeze from the east
and part of day with light breeze from the northwest

○ Clear
● Cloudy

Sextant

Section of a Maury
wind and current
chart showing
ships' tracks

Tsar, 1849
Young America, 1852
Stag Hound, 1851
Flora II, 1847
Sea Witch, 1848
Rainbow, 1850
Samuel Russell, 1850
Sea Queen, 1848
Sheffield, 1846

0.03
5°
0.02
0.10
125°
120°

Captain Josiah Creesy of
the *Flying Cloud*

The captain of a clipper was in complete command of ship, crew, and passengers. His word was absolute law. No one was allowed to enter his cabin but the steward who cleaned it, and the lee side of the poop deck was forbidden territory to everyone else on the ship; he walked there alone and spoke to the mates to give them orders or a reprimand.

Supervision was the captain's chief duty. He decided on the course to be sailed, and checked the mates' navigation. The mates could set more sail or shorten down on their own, but the captain could change their set-up with a word.

Every sailing day was divided into five four-hour watches and two two-hour watches. The first mate and the second mate, each with his half of the crew, took turns working a watch while the rest of the men relaxed, ate or slept. Each mate took charge during his watches; for those four hours or two hours it was his responsibility to see that his men kept sails and gear properly set and in good order.

The captain was the boss; the mates were the foremen; and the crew, the workers.

The mates could relax when they were not on watch, but the skipper was on duty day and night, and got little sleep if he was trying for a fast passage. But the rewards for his labor were good. If a clipper made it from New York or Boston to San Francisco in less than a hundred days, the owners paid the captain from $3000 to $5000, depending on the size of the ship and the value of the cargo.

Clipper with a moderate breeze on the starboard quarter

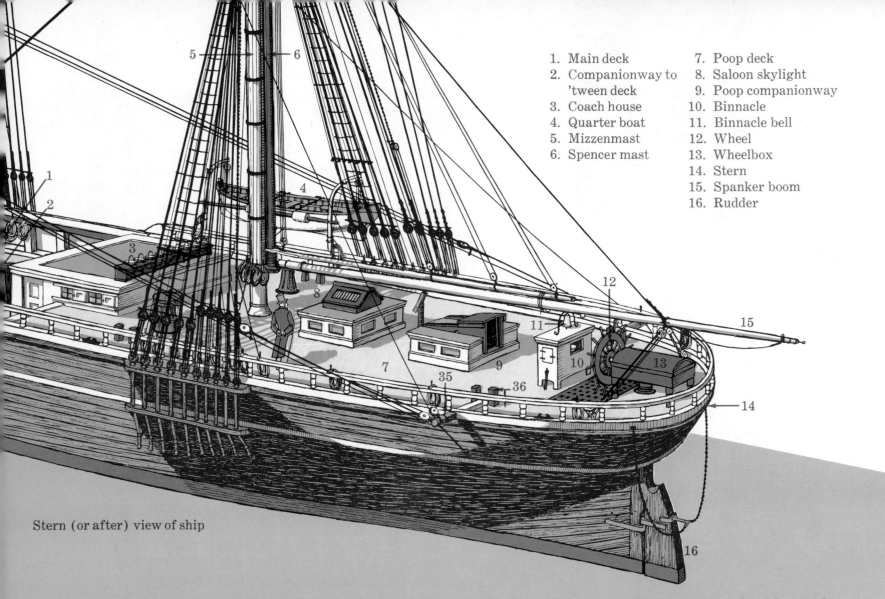

1. Main deck
2. Companionway to 'tween deck
3. Coach house
4. Quarter boat
5. Mizzenmast
6. Spencer mast
7. Poop deck
8. Saloon skylight
9. Poop companionway
10. Binnacle
11. Binnacle bell
12. Wheel
13. Wheelbox
14. Stern
15. Spanker boom
16. Rudder

Stern (or after) view of ship

The living quarters of captain, mates, and passengers were all located in the clipper's stern, or after section. The captain's cabin, on the starboard side, was the largest and most luxurious on the ship; it was equipped with sofa, desk, closet, washstand, and a large bunk—large enough to accommodate two, for some skippers took their wives to sea. The passengers' saloon was fitted with panels of rare wood, mirrors, sofas, and tables, and the staterooms for first-class passengers each held two double-decker bunks and a washstand. The bathroom had a wooden bathtub that could be filled with water through an opening in the deck.

The mizzenmast usually rose through the center

of the mess saloon, and around the mast was the mess table, which could be fitted with fiddles, or racks, to prevent dishes from sliding off in rough weather. The swivel dining-chairs were fastened to the deck to keep them from shifting.

The steward, who saw to it that the cook sent the better pieces of meat aft, served the captain, mates, and passengers. The pantry was his work-place. There he washed the glassware, silver and china, and stored the fancy foods, such as biscuits and jams, that were never seen in the crew's mess.

The first mate's cabin was furnished with a small sofa, a desk, a washstand, and a bunk. The second and third mates' rooms were smaller and had double-decker bunks. In the coach house were lockers for the officers' oilskins and foul-weather gear, as well as a large locker called the "slop chest," which was filled with clay pipes, smoking and chewing tobacco, shoes, socks, trousers, shirts, hats, jackets, boots, oilskins, and sou'wester hats. These were sold to the crew at less-than-shore prices.

Forward of the coach house was a hatch leading to the 'tween deck, where second-class passengers were put up in temporary bunks. On tables set up in their quarters, they ate the same food that was served all hands.

17. Keel
18. Hold
19. 'Tween deck
20. Slop chest
21. Passage
22. Oilskin locker
23. Passenger staterooms
24. Pantry
25. Dining saloon
26. 1st mate's cabin
27. 2nd mate's cabin
28. 3rd mate and steward
29. Saloon
30. Lockers
31. Captain
32. After passage
33. Officers' bathroom
34. Taffrail
35. Boomkins
36. Bitts

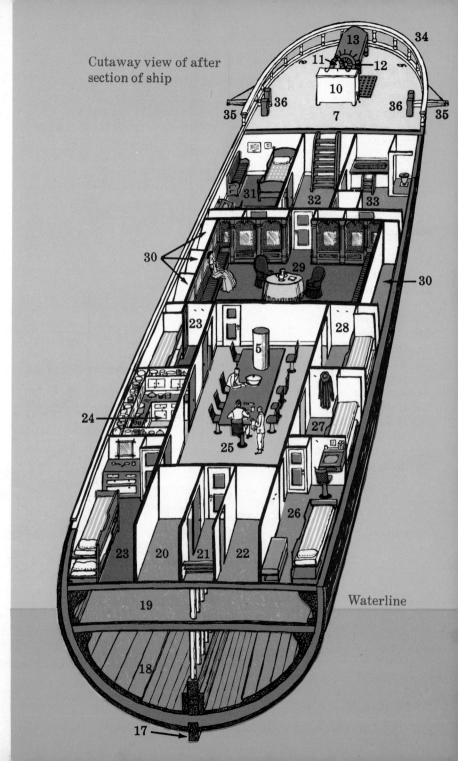

Cutaway view of after section of ship

Waterline

1. Fore-skysail stay
2. Foreroyal stay
3. Fore-topgallant stay
4. Outer jibstay
5. Jibstay
6. Forestay
7. Main-skysail stay
8. Main-royal stay
9. Main-topgallant stay
10. Main-topmast stay
11. Mainstay
12. Mizzen-skysail stay
13. Mizzen-royal stay
14. Mizzen-topgallant stay
15. Mizzen-topmast stay
16. Mizzen stay
17. Jibboom
18. Bowsprit
19. Martingale
20. Outer martingale stay
21. Inner martingale stay
22. Martingale backstay
23. Bobstays
24. Doublings
25. Mainmast
26. Main-topmast
27. Main-topgallant mast
28. Main-royal mast
29. Main yard
30. Main-topsail yard
31. Main-topgallant yard
32. Main-royal yard
33. Main-skysail yard
34. Main shrouds
35. Main-topmast shrouds
36. Main-topgallant shrouds
37. Main-topmast backstays
38. Main-topgallant backstays
39. Main-royal backstays
40. Main-skysail backstay
41. Maintop
42. Main-topmast crosstrees
43. Main-topmast stun'sl boom
44. Main-topgallant stun'sl boom
45. Main-royal stun'sl boom
46. Main-topsail yard tye
47. Main-topgallant yard tye
48. Main buntlines
49. Main-topsail buntlines
50. Main-topgallant buntline
51. Flemish horses
52. Ratlines
53. Footrope
54. Main-topsail sheets
55. Main yard lifts
56. Main-topmast yard lift
57. Main-topgallant sheets
58. Main-royal sheet
59. Main brace
60. Main-topsail braces
61. Main-topgallant braces
62. Bowlines
63. Fore-topsail braces
64. Fore-topgallant brace
65. Fore-royal brace
66. Main-topmast staysail halliard
67. Main-topgallant staysail halliard
68. Mizzen braces
69. Mizzen-topsail braces
70. Mizzen-topgallant braces
71. Mizzen-topgallant staysail halliard
72. Spanker gaff
73. Spanker boom
74. Spanker-boom lift
75. Spanker peak halliards
76. Spanker vang

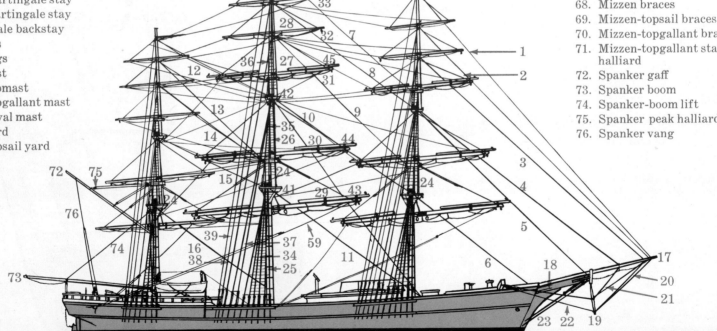

Partial rigging diagram of a clipper ship

Mainmast looking forward

Clipper ship under full sail

Names of clipper-ship sails

1. Flying jib
2. Outer jib
3. Inner jib
4. Main-royal staysail
5. Main-topgallant staysail
6. Main-topmast staysail
7. Mizzen-topgallant staysail
8. Spanker
9. Fore-skysail
10. Foreroyal
11. Fore-topgallant
12. Fore-topsail
13. Foresail
14. Main skysail
15. Main royal
16. Main-topgallant
17. Main topsail
18. Mainsail
19. Mizzen skysail
20. Mizzen royal
21. Mizzen-topgallant
22. Mizzen topsail
23. Cro'jack (furled)
24. Starboard foreroyal stun'sl
25. Starboard fore-topgallant stun'sl
26. Starboard fore-topmast stun'sl
27. Starboard lower fore-stun'sl
28. Port main-royal stun'sl
29. Starboard main-royal stun'sl
30. Port main-topgallant stun'sl
31. Starboard main-topgallant stun'sl
32. Starboard main-topmast stun'sl

The day on a clipper began at 4 A.M. First, all hands of the port watch had coffee in tin cups, while the first mate drank his from a china cup. The mate soon called out, "Turn to, forward, and wash down decks," and the boatswain rigged the head pump while the watch lifted all coils of line off the deck. Then, with trousers rolled up to the knees, the barefooted crew took up brooms and scrubbed the decks from bow to stern with sand sloshed about in salt water. This operation kept the decks clean but, more important, the water swelled the deck planks and prevented leaks onto the cargo below.

By this time, the sun was drying the lines, causing them to stretch a bit, so the watch tailed onto sheet, brace, and halliard, and got things shipshape and "Bristol fashion" with the help of a chantey. All brass-work had to be polished, all gear coiled up, paint and varnish wiped clear of rime, and the decks swabbed dry.

Now the captain came up for a morning sight through the sextant. The log chip was hove and the ship's speed calculated. Speed, position, and weather were noted in the logbook. At eight bells, or 8 A.M., the watch changed; the man or men at the wheel were relieved, a fresh look-out went to the forecastlehead, and breakfast was served to the men of the starboard watch, who then got down to checking all lines and gear. And when the hands were not making sail changes, they worked at the everlasting business of keeping the ship up.

At eight bells, or noon, the watch changed again, and the whole process was repeated. A twelve-hour workday was normal for everyone in the crew. But when emergencies came up in a gale, or if some gear broke down, all hands of both watches turned to until the problem was cleared up.

The mainmast from the
starboard side

1. Main truck
2. Main-skysail yard
3. Main-skysail yard lift
4. Footrope
5. Main-skysail braces
6. Main-royal braces
7. Mizzen-skysail braces
8. Mizzen-skysail stay
9. Mizzen-royal stay
10. Mizzen-topgallant braces
11. Main-topgallant braces
12. Main-topgallant stun'sl boom
13. Main-topsail yard
14. Mizzen-topgallant stay
15. Reef earing
16. Mizzen-topsail braces
17. Mizzen-topmast stay
18. Mizzen braces
19. Main-topsail clew line
20. Main yard lift
21. Main-topsail sheet
22. Main-topsail braces
23. Mizzen stay
24. Main-topmast stun'sl boom
25. Reef tackle
26. Main brace
27. Main-skysail backstay
28. Main-skysail halliard
29. Main-royal backstay
30. Main-topgallant backstay
31. Main-topmast backstays
32. Main shrouds
33. Port mainsheet
34. Quarter-deck rail
35. Quarter boat (*omitted*)
36. Main channels
37. Main chain plates
38. Scuppers
39. House flag of Higgins & Co.
40. Main skysail
41. Main-skysail clew line
42. Main-skysail mast
43. Main-royal yard
44. Main-royal yard lift
45. Main royal
46. Main-royal clew line
47. Main-royal mast
48. Fore-skysail braces
49. Fore-royal braces
50. Main-royal stun'sl boom
51. Main-royal stay
52. Main-royal staysail halliard
53. Main-skysail stay
54. Fore-topgallant braces
55. Main-topgallant yard lift
56. Main-topgallant
57. Main-topgallant clew line
58. Main-topgallant mast
59. Main-topgallant shrouds
60. Main-topmast crosstrees
61. Starboard main-topgallant bowline
62. Footrope
63. Flemish horse
64. Main-topsail yard lift
65. Main-topgallant mast stay
66. Main-topgallant staysail halliard
67. Fore-topsail braces
68. Main topsail
69. Main-topsail clew line
70. Main-topmast
71. Main-topmast shrouds
72. Maintop
73. Starboard main-topsail bowline
74. Main yard
75. Starboard main buntlines
76. Reef points
77. Main-topmast stay
78. Main-topmast staysail halliard
79. Forebrace
80. Mainsail
81. Main clew garnets
82. Starboard mainsheet
83. Mainmast
84. Boat
85. Main tack
86. Mainstay
87. Starboard main bowline
88. Rigging deadeyes

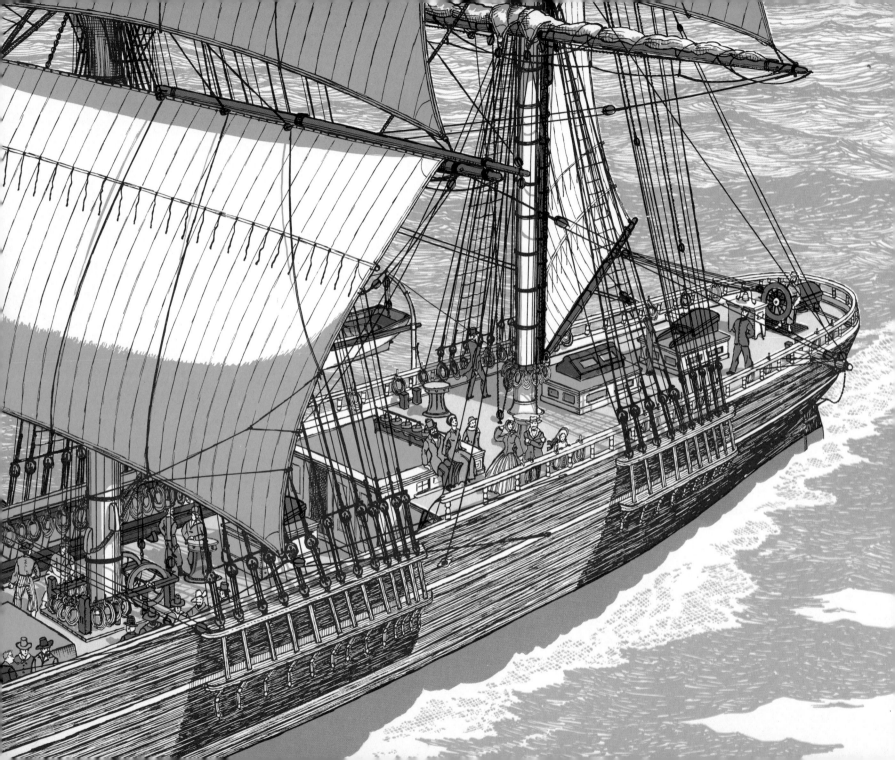

The binnacle is a box that protects and houses the compass. In it are oil lamps to illuminate the compass at night, and on top of it is the bell that was rung every half hour. On the side facing the helmsman is a door with sliding shutters, through which the man at the wheel could see the compass. The compass bowl rests on gimbals that keep it level as the ship rolls and pitches.

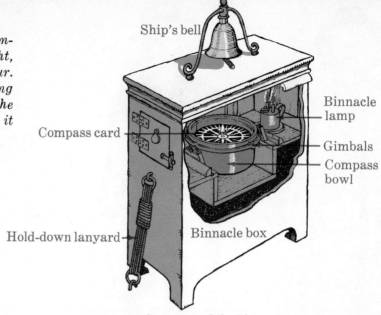

Cutaway of the binnacle

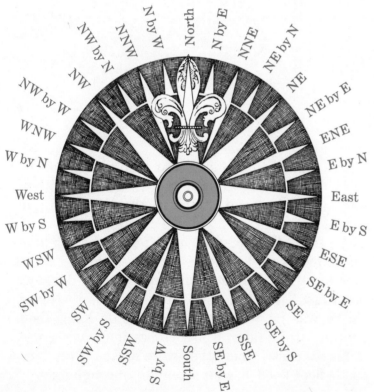

Compass card and the points of the compass

The best clipper-ship sailors were "packet rats," men of English, Irish or Welsh extraction who had sailed on the packet ships that ran between American and English ports. These men were wild, rough types who understood no law but force. They were dirty, uncouth, ignorant brutes and bullies, but they were superb sailors and feared neither man nor weather. A few professional foremast-hands were native Americans who, for one reason or another, had not made the quarter-deck. They usually resented their failure and became "sea lawyers"—great talkers and arguers who caused much discontent among the crew. Some hands were itinerant laborers trying to work their way to the gold fields. And there were many foreigners who barely understood orders, most of them deserters from French, Dutch, Greek, Italian, German, Scandinavian, Russian, and Spanish ships.

Foul-weather gear   Fair-weather gear

Officers' dress was informal. They wore civilian clothes on shore, and at sea wore old clothes, heavy or light, according to the weather. The crew wore cheap or second-hand clothes that were more patches than pants after a long voyage. When a button was lost, a wooden toggle replaced it. In wet weather all hands wore oilskins (raincoats soaked in raw oil to make them waterproof) and sou'wester hats (broad-brimmed hats that came down low at the back to keep out rain and sea water). Sea boots were made of oiled leather. "Soul and body lashings" (strings tied around sleeves and cuffs) kept rain and spray from trickling in.

The crew's quarters were cramped and uncomfortable. Forecastles were wet in heavy weather, unbearably hot and stuffy in the tropics. Light came from one reeking whale-oil lamp.

A sailor's bed (2 feet by 6 feet) was made of rough pine boards, and his mattress was a canvas sack of straw, known to all sailors as a "donkey's breakfast." Vermin of all sorts infested the place. There was no way to dry clothes or hang them neatly. All of a sailor's poor possessions were stored in his sea chest, where they were soaked if the forecastle floor flooded, as it often did in rough seas.

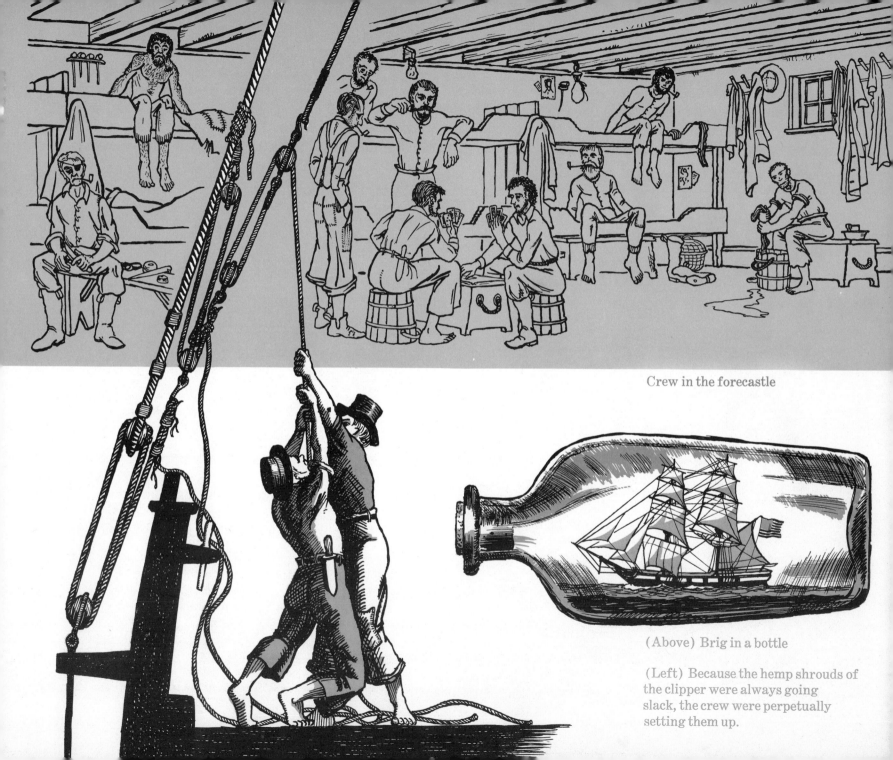

Crew in the forecastle

(Above) Brig in a bottle

(Left) Because the hemp shrouds of the clipper were always going slack, the crew were perpetually setting them up.

On a clipper—and on other sailing ships until the end of the sailing days—the life of the man "before the mast" was hard. He was encouraged in his duties by kicks and curses from the mates—and woe to any hand caught shirking his tasks. The hard work was endless and, in bad weather, extremely hazardous.

There were dozens of jobs of sailorizing to be done on a ship: overhauling ratlines; reeving off new lines; seizing, worming, parcelling and serving; making and installing chafing gear; picking old rope into oakum; overhauling and painting the anchor chain, etc., etc., ad infinitum. And if the decks were not absolutely clean, they had to be holystoned. On hands and knees, with a porous stone about the size of a Bible—using sand as an abrasive and water as a lubricant—the men scoured the decks until they were white.

Painted trim had to be rubbed with damp canvas and fine sand until it was as smooth as velvet. The shrouds and stays were tightened and tarred—and too bad for the unfortunate sailor, aloft in a swinging boatswain's chair, who spilled a drop of tar on a sail or deck.

Never an idle moment for the crew of a clipper, and no Sundays off or holidays at sea.

Midnight

First watch

Middle watch

Second dogwatch

Morning watch

Supper

First dog watch

PM AM

Supper

Afternoon watch

Forenoon watch

Breakfast

Noon
Dinner

The small circled figures are the number of bells struck each half hour.

The boldface numbers are the hours of the day.

Time at sea is divided into five four-hour watches that run from 8 P.M. to 4 P.M., and two dogwatches (4 to 6 P.M. and 6 to 8 P.M.). Let's say that a ship goes to sea on a Monday night. The port watch, under the first mate, stands the first watch, 8 P.M. to midnight. The starboard watch, under the second mate, stands the middle watch on Tuesday, midnight to 4 A.M., and has breakfast after going off duty. The port watch has breakfast before going on duty to stand the morning watch, 4 to 8 A.M. The starboard watch stands the forenoon watch, 8 A.M. to noon, and has dinner after going off watch. The port watch, which has dinner before noon, stands both the afternoon watch and the first dogwatch, noon to 6 P.M. The starboard watch has supper at 5 P.M. and takes both the second dogwatch and first watch, from 6 P.M. to midnight. The port watch has supper at 6 P.M. and is free until midnight, when they take the Wednesday middle watch, and so on.

Every half hour the bells are rung: one bell at 12:30 A.M. or P.M.; two bells at 1 A.M. or P.M.; three bells at 1:30 A.M. or P.M. and so on. (See diagram.)

The man at the wheel hears the bells on the ship's clock in the after passage, and rings the bell on the binnacle. The lookout on watch on the forecastlehead repeats the rings on the bell there, which can be heard throughout the ship.

Reefing the main topsail

The food served to the crew was monotonous and, worse, it was prepared by an incompetent cook—nicknamed "the doctor" because he doctored up such horrible messes.

The amount of food was adequate. Each week, every hand was allowed 7 pounds of hardtack (bread); 6 pounds of salt beef (corned beef), known as salt horse; 3¾ pounds of pickled pork; 1½ pounds of flour; 3½ pints of dried peas or beans; ⅞ ounces of tea; 3½ ounces of coffee, which was mostly chicory and usually had a dead cockroach or two in it; 14 ounces of sugar or molasses; and 5 gallons, 1 quart of water (equal to 3 quarts of water a day). The drinking water was kept in a large iron tank in the hold, forward of the mainmast, and it was stringy and green with algae before the ship left the tropics on a round-the-Horn voyage. Its taste can be left to the imagination.

The "mess cooks," elected each week from among the watch, carried the food from the galley to the crew's living quarters in piggins, or oval tubs; they carted the hardtack on a wooden tray called the bread barge. Beef or pork was ladled out into tin plates, and the men ate with sheath knives and spoons while squatting on the deck or sitting on a sea chest. Coffee and tea were poured into tin cups from a can with a handle on it. Everyone had to take his coffee or tea sweet or not at all; molasses or sugar was added in the galley so that all hands would get an equal amount of sweets.

In the tropics, flying fish often landed on deck. These belonged to the captain and the mates, according to ship's law, but they made a welcome

The wooden water cask, or scuttle butt, was filled with the ship's daily water ration from the tank in the hold. Members of the crew went to it to drink and gossip. Hence, rumor and gossip acquired the slang name "scuttlebutt."

treat when stolen and fried. An occasional dolphin was speared by a man on the bowsprit, and made a fine baked snack for the watch.

From time to time, there was a special treat: "dandy funk" (baked, broken hardtack covered with molasses) or "plum duff" (raisins or prunes, flour, fat and molasses boiled in a bag). If these were served twice a month, the ship was considered a gourmet's dream.

A man who was sick with indigestion or who "just didn't feel right" could have a dose of salts or ipecac—kill or cure. Broken limbs were set by the mates or the captain in a rough-and-ready way, but if a man had appendicitis, he died. There were very few old sailors—a man of fifty before the mast was rare. The survivors often became cooks who sauced the food with hate and malice.

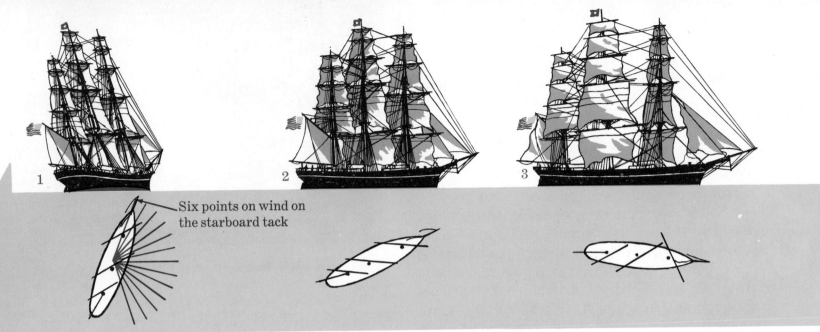

Six points on wind on the starboard tack

Clipper ship beating to windward

"Knowing the ropes" was a vital part of every hand's training, especially when it was necessary to tack, or come about. Each man had to know exactly what he must do at every step.

The ship was close-hauled (position 1) on the starboard tack (wind coming over the right bow, yards braced at an angle of 30 degrees to the ship's central axis). When the mate commanded, "Ready about," the men made ready to cast off tacks, sheets, braces, and bowlines.

At the command, "Helm's a-lee," the rudder was turned to starboard, then the port foresheet, port forebraces, starboard bowlines, port forestaysail sheet, and port jib sheets were cast off; the ship luffed up into the wind (position 2).

When the mainsails and mizzen sails began to shake, the command, "Off tacks and sheets," was given. The men would cast off the port, main and mizzen sheets, braces, and starboard bowlines and tacks; the yards on the mainmast and mizzenmast would then swing around from the force of the wind (position 3).

The mate now shouted, "Mainsail haul"; starboard main and mizzen sheets and braces were pulled taut, and the port tacks were hauled in. The wind on the backed foresails and jibs pushed the bow to starboard until the ship was about six points off the wind on the port tack.

The command, "Let go and haul," rang out. The port foresheet and braces were eased (slacked slowly), and the yards swung around in line with those of the mainmast and mizzenmast. The port

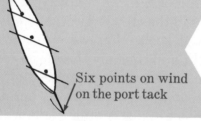

Wind direction

Six points on wind on the port tack

foretack, starboard foresheet, starboard braces, starboard sheet of forestaysail, and starboard sheets of the jibs were hauled taut (position 4). Finally, the men hauled the port bowlines and port braces (pulled them taut), coiled the gear and hung it on the pins.

Considering the hard work and hardships, it is difficult to understand why anybody in his right mind went to sea. Perhaps sailors were drawn by the mystery and beauty of it all. On a quiet night watch, when the ship was sailing in the glitter of moonlight, there came such a feeling of pride and accomplishment, even to the lowest ship's boy, that it helped to make up for the bad food and aching backs.

The pleasures of the men before the mast were few, and because they were so few they were gloried in. Crossing the line (the equator) was one excuse for a revel. At eight bells in the afternoon watch, Father Neptune, his wife Amphitrite, and their retinue "came aboard," and the god of the ocean asked for his sons who had not yet received his blessing. The men who were crossing the equator for the first time were lined up near the mainmast, with a big tub of water close by, and then Neptune asked the captain if he had any green hands aboard who needed a shave. One at a time, the new men were seated on the edge of the tub, lathered with a vile mess of tar, soapsuds, and grease, and shaved with a huge razor made from an iron barrel-hoop. When scraped, each man was flipped over into the tub of water and then handed a sack smeared with black paint to use as a towel.

Of course, Father Neptune, his wife, and attendants were members of the crew dressed up in rope-yarn beards and wild costumes. All hands and the cook joined in the fun. Even the captain welcomed Neptune and company aboard, probably the only time he spoke directly to a foremasthand during the entire voyage.

Some men found time to play checkers on a board made of canvas stretched over a piece of wood. The checkers were a broomstick sawed into discs about a quarter of an inch thick; a nail was driven through each one so that the point could stick into the checkerboard and allow the men to play in a high wind. There were always a few greasy decks of cards in the crew's forecastle, and a few ancient dog-eared books that were devoured, when there was light and time, by those who could read.

Then there was the everlasting pastime of yarning. Great tales—true, false, heroic, and tragic—were told while standing night watches out of the mate's earshot.

Seeing another clipper under sail always made a man realize how magnificent his own ship must be; it was a sight that gave all hands a sense of proud participation, a special feeling no landsman can understand until he is on a ship under sail at sea.

Perhaps the mysteriousness of the sea is its attraction. We know what makes the winds blow, and the whys and wherefores of waves; but when you are out on the sea, all the knowledge in the world does not detract from the majesty and wonder of it.

In a hurricane, a hand on a clipper suddenly realized his helplessness and insignificance. With good management the ship would come through, perhaps, but it was often a question of luck. And no man could possibly feel safe in a dense fog. Near shore there was the danger of rocks and reefs, and far out at sea even the best foghorns and whistles were not always heard. Ships could crash into each other and lose all hands.

The list of ships missing from unknown causes or disasters is long and terrifying. Some might have capsized in a violent and sudden squall. Others might have foundered because they were sailed under the water by a hard-driving master; others might have hit an iceberg or half-submerged derelict; some might have caught fire from spontaneous combustion in the cargo; lightning might have been the end of others; or, most horrible of all, disease might have killed everyone on board while the ship sailed on and on.

But the perils of the sea did not make the men who loved the clippers stay at home. They sailed, and their clippers served a valuable purpose. They helped to bring the opposite shores of our country closer together. They increased the respect for American ships in maritime nations all over the world. They set records for fast passages that steamships were decades in bettering.

Because of the competition for fast passages, the clippers, in their prime, were driven harder and

harder; masts, rigging, and hull were overstrained, and the ships became old and worn out long before their time.

The clippers were a great success from 1850 to 1855, but as the gold rush dwindled and speed became less important, the slower, bulkier ships began to compete successfully.

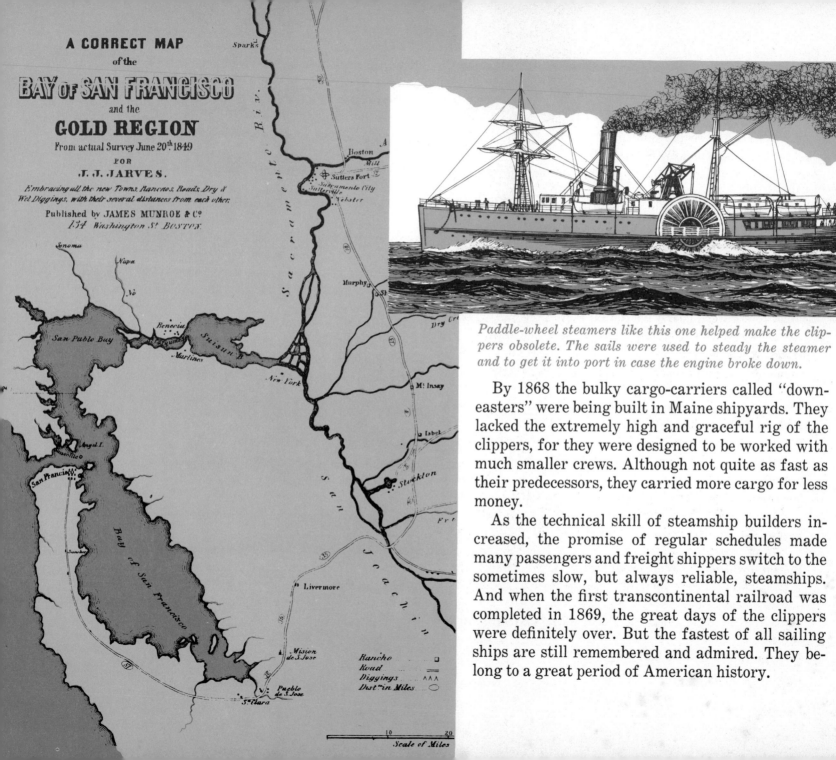

A CORRECT MAP

of the

BAY of SAN FRANCISCO

and the

GOLD REGION

From actual Survey June 20th 1849

FOR

J. J. JARVES.

Embracing all the new Towns, Ranchos, Roads, Dry & Wet Diggings, with their several distances from each other.

Published by JAMES MUNROE & C?
134 Washington St BOSTON.

Paddle-wheel steamers like this one helped make the clippers obsolete. The sails were used to steady the steamer and to get it into port in case the engine broke down.

By 1868 the bulky cargo-carriers called "downeasters" were being built in Maine shipyards. They lacked the extremely high and graceful rig of the clippers, for they were designed to be worked with much smaller crews. Although not quite as fast as their predecessors, they carried more cargo for less money.

As the technical skill of steamship builders increased, the promise of regular schedules made many passengers and freight shippers switch to the sometimes slow, but always reliable, steamships. And when the first transcontinental railroad was completed in 1869, the great days of the clippers were definitely over. But the fastest of all sailing ships are still remembered and admired. They belong to a great period of American history.

GLOSSARY

Definitions of special words and terms which are not fully explained in text and pictures.

aft. Toward the rear, or stern, of a ship.

algae. Seaweeds and sea mosses.

all hands. All the working members of the ship's company.

ballast. Stones or other heavy material stored in the hold to stabilize the ship when there is little cargo.

before the mast. Refers to ordinary sailors, who lived in the forecastle, in front of the mainmast.

belaying pins. The wooden or iron pins to which lines could be attached.

bilge. The lowest, nearly horizontal part of the hull, where dirt and water could collect and cause a foul smell.

block. A wooden pulley.

boatswain. A petty officer in charge of sails, rigging, and anchors.

boatswain's chair. A flat piece of wood slung on a rope and used as a chair while up in the rigging.

bowline. A rope attached to the middle of the perpendicular edge of a square sail; it keeps the sail taut when going to windward.

bowsprit. A spar projecting forward from the bow; the jibs and stays are fastened to it.

braces. Lines attached to the outer ends of the yards so they can be moved about.

Bristol fashion. In good order; ships from Bristol, the English port, were thought to be the neatest and cleanest vessels.

cast off. To let go, release a line from a belaying pin or cleat.

ceiling. A ship's inner planking.

chafing gear. The covering of a line or spar that prevents wear.

chanteyman. The leader of the chantey.

chicory. A root ground for use with or instead of coffee.

China-tea clipper. A fast, small-to-medium-sized ship that sailed to China for tea.

chronometer. A very accurate clock used for determining longitude at sea.

close-hauled. Sailing as close against the wind as the vessel will go.

coach house. The deckhouse at the break of the poop.

coil. A length of rope arranged in concentric circles.

drive. To carry so much sail that a ship is hard-pressed; this can be carried so far that the ship is driven under the water and sinks.

forecastle. A short raised deck at the bow; also, the forward deckhouse where the crew slept.

foremasthands. *See* before the mast.

foretack. The ropes by which the lower corners of the square forecourse are held and hauled.

forward. The front part of the ship.

frames. The ribs or skeleton of a ship.

gear. The rigging in general.

gear coiled on pins. Running rigging coiled neatly and hung on belaying pins.

green hands. Untrained sailors.

halliards. The ropes and tackle for raising and lowering the spars or sails.

hands. The crew.

hardtack. A large round biscuit baked without salt.

hatch. An opening in a deck, usually square or oblong.

head pump. A pump up forward used to water down the decks.

heave to. To turn into the wind so that the ship loses forward motion.

helm. Wheel by which the rudder is turned.

hull. The body of a vessel, exclusive of spars and sails.

ipecac. A drug used to induce vomiting.

Jacob's ladder. A rope ladder with wooden rungs.

jib. The triangular staysail set from outer end of jib-boom to fore-topmast head.

keel. The lowest longitudinal timber of a vessel, on which the framework of the hull is built.

knees. Pieces of timber with natural angles, used in ship construction to strengthen corners.

knot. One nautical mile per hour; a nautical mile equals 1-1/7 land miles.

lazaret. The after part of the hold, used as a storeroom.

learn the ropes. To commit to memory every rope and its function.

lee. The side away from the wind.

line. A rope used for some specific purpose.

lines of a ship. The outlines from bow to stern, from keel to sheer strake, and of the ship's sections.

logbook. A daily record of the distance sailed, the course and the weather.

log chip. A triangular weighted board attached to the log line, which is knotted every 47′ 3″. When the log chip is heaved overboard, the number of knots that run out in 28 seconds shows the ship's speed.

luff. To bring the bow nearer the wind.

maritime nations. Countries, usually with ports on the sea, engaged in shipping.

marlin. Very strong, two-stranded string soaked in Stockholm tar.

oakum. Old rope picked to pieces, soaked in Stockholm tar, and then used to caulk seams.

packet ships. Fast-sailing ships that crossed the Atlantic on regular schedules.

parcelling. *See* worming.

pilot. A qualified guide who takes charge of conducting a ship in or out of port.

pins. *See* belaying pins.

planking. Curved pieces of wood that make up the ship's outer skin.

poop deck. The raised section of deck at the stern.

port. The left side of the ship, looking forward.

quarter-deck. *See* poop deck.

ratlines. Small ropes fastened across ship's shrouds like ladder rungs.

raw oil. Uncooked linseed oil.

reef point. One of the short ropes attached to a sail, used to shorten sail in high winds.

reeve off. To thread rope through a block.

rime. The salt left when sea spray dries.

running rigging. Ropes and lines used to raise, lower, and control sails.

seize. To lash or fasten with several turns of cord.

serving. *See* worming.

set up the rigging. To tighten shrouds and stays.

sextant. An instrument used for measuring altitudes at sea so as to find latitude.

sheath knife. A daggerlike knife worn in a leather sheath, hung from the belt in back so as to be out of the way when aloft.

sheet. A rope or chain which regulates the angle at which a sail is set in relation to the wind.

spars. A general term for masts, yards, booms, or gaffs.

spontaneous combustion. Fire caused by natural chemical action.

standing rigging. Fixed shrouds and stays.

starboard. The right side of a ship, looking forward.

stay. A rope supporting a mast or spar.

Stockholm tar. A tar prepared from resinous pine wood, used as a preservative.

stow. To pack goods with a minimum waste of space.

tack. To change direction by shifting the helm and sails so that the wind strikes the sails on the other side, to take a zigzag course.

tack. A rope holding the forward lower corner of a sail.

tail on. To pick up a rope and pull it.

tarred lines. Rigging smeared or painted with Stockholm tar.

watch below. Time when the crew is off duty.

ways (ship ways). Long slanting beams, leading from shore to sea, from which a ship can be launched or on which it can be hauled out.

windward. In the direction from which the wind blows.

worming, parcelling, and serving. Methods for protecting ropes and cables from chafe and weather: to worm, small ropes are laid in the spiral grooves of a larger rope; to parcel, canvas is wrapped around the wormed rope; to serve, marlin is wrapped very tightly around the wormed and parcelled rope.

yard. A cylindrical spar slung horizontally across the mast to support a square sail.

ACKNOWLEDGMENTS

The author gratefully acknowledges that most of his research was done at the following museums:

The Museum of Fine Arts, Boston, Massachusetts; U. S. National Museum, Washington, D.C.; The Marine Historical Association, Mystic, Connecticut; San Francisco Maritime Museum, San Francisco, California; Musee de la Marine, Paris, France; Science Museum, London, England; The Mariner's Museum, Newport News, Virginia.

BIBLIOGRAPHY

The following books and magazines were valuable sources of information in the preparation of *Clipper Ship:*

Abell, Sir Westcott. *The Shipwright's Trade.* Cambridge, England: Cambridge University Press, 1948.

American Neptune Magazine. January 1947; January 1959; and April 1959.

Clarke, Arthur H. *The Clipper Ship Era.* New York: G. P. Putnam's Sons, 1910.

Cutler, Carl C. *Greyhounds of the Sea.* New York: G. P. Putnam's Sons, 1930.

Durant, John and Alice. *Pictorial History of American Ships.* New York: A. S. Barnes and Co., Inc., 1953.

Judson, Clara Ingram. *Donald McKay.* New York: Charles Scribner's Sons, 1943.

Knight, Austin M. *Modern Seamanship.* New York: D. Van Nostrand Co., Inc., 1901.

Laing, Alexander. *The Sea Witch.* New York: Murray Hill Books, 1944.

Lubbock, Basil. *The China Clippers.* Glasgow, Scotland: James Brown & Sons, 1916.

Lubbock, Basil. *The Last of the Windjammers.* Boston: Charles E. Laurait, 1927.

Meader, Stephen W. *The Voyage of the Javelin.* New York: Harcourt, Brace & World, Inc., 1959.

Riesenberg, Felix. *Standard Seamanship for the Merchant Service.* New York: D. Van Nostrand Co., Inc., 1922.

Riesenberg, Felix. *Under Sail, A Boy's Voyage Around Cape Horn.* New York: The Macmillan Company, 1918.

Villiers, Alan. *The Set of the Sails.* New York: Charles Scribner's Sons, 1949.